The Home Bible Study Series was first published in the United Kingdom for the fellowship at Moment of Truth Ministries.

All Bible quotations are taken from the Authorised King James Version.

DEDICATION

The Home Bible Study Series is dedicated to all the apostles and believers of the early Church, who were faithful to the call, mission and doctrine of Christ and who willingly sealed their testimony for Christ's Church with their very blood.

The heritage and legacy they left behind cannot be quantified. Without their awesome dedication to truth, the cause of Christ would have long been buried by the never relenting wiles of satan. We thank the Almighty God for the great price they paid.

Their faithfulness, however, stands as a great challenge for present day believers. We need to be devoted to truth as they were. It is with great disbelief and pain we continue to witness satan's unhindered infiltration of mainstream Churches with damnable error and heresies.
May the Lord give us the 'steel' that we witnessed in the early Church to stand for the truth and resist all kinds of falsehood with a holy, yet loving, determination.

We would like to thank all who contributed towards the work of volume one, most especially those who spent so many hours proofreading and editing this piece of work. Our prayer is that all who have contributed in one way or the other to this volume will never lose their reward of service in Jesus Name.

May the Lord keep us faithful to His unchanging truth.

Samson Jebutu

TABLE OF CONTENTS

THE SECRET OF REVIVAL:
START A HOME GROUP NOW!

Do you know that the early believers did not have a single Church building for more than 200 years after Pentecost? History tells us that the first Church building was found at Dura Europos on the Euphrates, dating about 231 years after Christ's death. How then did the Church survive? Well, rather than gather together to worship in a main building once a week, they met locally in houses to pray, study and fellowship together.

This is the very heart of **The Home Bible School Series**. This booklet is meant to inspire Christians to go back to the blueprint given by God and start home groups all over the world where people can meet locally to study, pray and exhort one another. It is a tragedy that we spend so much time and investment on one 'grand service' a week and miss out on true revival that comes through local home groups who come together for concentrated study, prayers and fellowship.

The believers literally took the words of Christ to heart when He said in Matthew 18:20 **'For where two or three are gathered together in my name, there am I in the midst of them.'** Consequently, they did not wait for major buildings to start Christian fellowship. They had them in their homes! There is an amazing power God has invested in home groups. Home groups led to the Church's exponential growth as believers met in houses (Acts 2:46).

Aquila and Priscilla had a Church in their house (I Corinthians 16:19). When Peter was imprisoned by Herod, the Church prayed one of the most amazing prayers in the house of Mary (Acts 12:12). It was at Cornelius' house that the Gentiles first received the Holy Spirit (Acts 10:22–24). For two whole years Paul the Apostle hired a house to receive all that would come to listen to the gospel (Acts 28:30).

With this material in your hand, you have a great opportunity to start a home group and be an instrument of revival in your locality. May the Lord use you to gather other people at His feet for study, prayer and fellowship. William Beckham once said;

The strongest organizational unit in the world's history would appear) be that which we call a cell (home group) because it is a remorseless elf-multiplier; is exceptionally difficult to destroy; can preserve its ıtensity of local life while vast organizations quickly wither when they re weakened at the centre; can defy the power of governments; is the ppropriate lever of prising open any status quo.' [1]

'ou can start another revival right in your home...why wait?

'he Home Bible Study Series

---

[1] *Herbert Butterfield, quoted in William Beckham, The Two Winged Church Will Fly (Houston: Touch Publications, 1993), 119.*

SAMPLE OF A HOME GROUP SCHEDULE

- Opening Prayer
- Songs & Hymns
- Testimonies from Home Group members
- Prayer Sessions based on the needs of Home Group members
- Group Study
- Closing Prayer / Benediction

LESSON 1

WHAT IS SALVATION?

TEXT: Titus 2: 11 – 14; Romans 10: 12, 13; Acts 4:12

Salvation is the most fundamental experience of every genuine believer and therefore it is not surprising that the word 'salvation' is commonly used in Christendom. However, 'salvation' can mean different things to different people. Some believe, for instance, that salvation is just a confession of faith (or a mental assent of the finished work of Christ). Others see salvation as an escape route from hell, while some see salvation as merely outward rituals, consisting of good works carried out through man's effort. In spite of the multiple perceptions and definitions we have today, it is so important for the sincere seeker to understand what the scriptures say about salvation and how to experience the same.

1. Read Titus 2: 11 – 14.
   These verses contain one of the most comprehensive definitions of salvation you can find in the Bible. What does each verse tell you about the 'components' of salvation?

2. Read 2 Corinthians 5: 17. Explain in what ways genuine salvation affects the 'old life'.

3. Paul mentions the phrase 'POWER OF GOD' in his statement of Romans 1:16 '**I am not ashamed of the gospel of Christ: for it is the power of God unto salvation to everyone that believeth; to the Jew first, and also to the Greek'.** What does the power of God actually do at salvation?

4. Read Galatians 2:17. If we are truly saved and have been touched by the power of God, is it still possible to remain under the yoke, bondage and dominion of sin and be at the mercy of the 'old life'?

Note:
According to Scripture, salvation is a very radical experience carried out by God's grace on sincere seekers. The experience of salvation empowers the believer to have total victory over the 'old life' of sin and live in the newness of life. Romans Chapter 6, best describes the outcome of genuine salvation.

5. Read Romans 6: 4 – 6. You will notice that in relation to salvation, the writer talks about death and life (or crucifixion and resurrection). What exactly dies (or is crucified) at salvation and what comes to life (or is resurrected) at salvation?

6. Read John 3:16; John 1:29, 36 and I John 3:5. Why is Jesus Christ central to the salvation of the believer in relation to our past sins?

7. Read John 1: 12; II Corinthians 5: 17; John 8: 34 – 36. Why is Jesus Christ central to the salvation of the believer in relation to receiving the power to live in the newness of life?

Note:
The reason why a simple prayer of confession does not seem to do any good for the modern-day professors of Christianity is because many in the church do not fully understand what they are actually praying for! The preaching and prayer of salvation covers four main areas:

- Acknowledging one's sinfulness and a sincere repentance from sin.
- Asking for the forgiveness of past sins and iniquities.
- Accepting that Christ died for those sins in our place and that Christ took our own punishment.
- Asking the Lord **to empower the believer to live a new life through Christ.**

Unfortunately, it is on the fourth point that many miss out! They pray on the first three points but never experience true salvation because no one can live in NEWNESS OF LIFE (not modification of the old-life) without divine empowerment from above.

8. Read Romans 10: 9 – 13. What really is the believer saved from at the point of genuine salvation?

9. Read Acts 4: 12. Explain the meaning of this verse.

10. What is the implication of this verse (Acts 4:12) to professors of other religions?

Therefore if any man be in Christ, he is a new creation: old things are passed away; behold all things are become new (II Corinthians 5: 17).

Remember ALL THINGS ARE BECOME NEW! Amen.

LESSON 2

WE ARE FORGIVEN TO FORGIVE OTHERS

MAIN TEXT: Matthew 18: 21 – 35; Mark 11: 24 – 26

One of the greatest attributes of God is His tender mercy towards those He forgives. The Christian faith is about forgiveness. It is about a loving Father who provides a door of mercy and forgiveness to those who seek Him sincerely.

Every true believer is a recipient of God's forgiveness. What a peace! What a joy! What blessed assurance! How wonderful it is to hear those re-assuring words from the lips of the Holy Spirit: 'Blessed is he whose transgression is forgiven, whose sin is covered' (Psalm 32:1). There is a mysterious, yet soothing harmony within the heart of the believer who has tasted of God's forgiveness and the magnitude of His grace.

The Psalmist says;

For thou, Lord, art good, and ready to forgive; and plenteous in mercy unto all them that call upon thee. (Psalm 86:5)

However, with God's forgiveness comes the great responsibility, for all believers, to exemplify true sonship through Christ by forgiving all who offend them irrespective of the magnitude of the offence. Recipients of God's grace of forgiveness must correspondingly be givers of the same grace.

The radiance of the God-given life will never truly shine in us if we do not have the grace to forgive. Unforgiveness is a serious blemish that grieves the Holy Spirit and is unacceptable in the courts of heaven. This lesson will examine the importance of forgiveness and the dangers that awaits those who dare to do otherwise.

1. Why do you think Peter asked the question about forgiveness in Matthew 18:21?

. What did Jesus Christ mean by 'seventy times seven' in Matthew 18:22?

. Who do the following characters represent in the parable?

- The first servant - the one who was forgiven by the king (Matthew 18:24 - 27).
- The second servant - the one who asked for forgiveness from the first servant (Matthew 18:28 – 30).

Note:

You will notice that what the second servant owed the first servant was nothing in comparison with what the first servant owed the king.

To put it in perspective, the first servant owed the king 10,000 talents which in today's calculation is between 1 – 2 billion pounds sterling. Jesus used such an extraordinary amount in this parable to underscore the fact that the first servant owed the king an amount he could never pay back in his life time. In fact it would have taken him about 200,000 years to pay back the debt based on the wages current at the time.

On the other hand, what the second servant owed the first servant was just an hundred pence which in today's calculation is about £10. Yet the first servant who had obtained such great forgiveness and mercy from the king could not give the same to a fellow servant!

This is the way the Lord views professing believers who refuse to forgive others even though they themselves have been recipients of God's forgiveness. God sees such people as unmerciful servants! Unforgiveness reflects a deeper problem within the heart. It is mark of a counterfeit or wavering Christian experience.

4. What is the consequence of unforgiveness in Matthew 18: 32 – 35?

5. The fact that Jesus was relating this parable to His disciples tells u something. What is it?

Note:

Jesus ends that parable by saying that we ought to forgive from the heart. Go knows when a person has forgiven from the heart. He also knows when we ar just acting before men but have not truly forgiven from the heart.

6. What does it mean to forgive from the heart?

7. What is the relationship between forgiveness and receiving answer to prayers? Please read Mark 11: 24 – 26 for your answer.

8. What does Colossians 3: 13 tell us about forgiveness?

9. On what occasion(s) have you found it difficult to forgive and how did you overcome it?

10. You will notice that in Luke 17: 3, 4 it is the 'offended' that Jesus is telling to take heed and not the offender. Why is this?

To forgive is to set a prisoner free and discover the prisoner was you —
Unknown author

LESSON 3

THE PARABLE OF THE FIG-TREE
MAIN TEXT: LUKE 13: 6-9

The parable of the fig tree is a parable of great importance. Although very short, the underlying message of this parable is very profound. Jesus Christ, in this parable, underscores the importance of bearing fruit. God has not merely called us to attend church services, sing, share testimonies and preach the word routinely. The primary calling of the believer is to bear fruit.

One of Jesus Christ's most notable statements at the Mount is: ***'Wherefore by their fruits ye shall know them'*** Matthew 7:20. A person's true identity is revealed not by what he or she professes but by the kind of fruit produced.

Paul, in harmony with the Lord's message, reiterated the same in his epistle to Titus: ***'They profess that they know God; but in works (fruit) they deny Him, being abominable, and disobedient, and unto every good work reprobate'*** (Titus 1:16).

The truth revealed throughout Scripture is that God never calls His people to religion but to a ***'fruit-bearing life'.*** Consequently, through this parable, Jesus Christ once again emphasises the need for the true believer to bear fruit. This is the major thing God looks for in His children.

We unfortunately live at a time when, fruit-bearing has been relegated to the background. It is practically treated as inconsequential and appears to have been exchanged for a one-minute confession, church-attendance, church activities, denominational commitment, self-works and empty profession. May the Lord give us ears to hear what the Spirit is saying at this critical time through the parable of the fig-tree.

1. Why do you think Jesus Christ gave this parable?

2. There are copious examples in Scripture (in both the Old and the New Testaments) where God likens people to trees. Please give some of these examples.

3. Compare this parable with Isaiah 5: 1 – 7 and explain how it is similar to the parable in this lesson.

Note:
God repetitively likens human beings to trees throughout Scripture.

In Psalm 1: 3 we are told:
'And he (the righteous) shall be like a tree planted by the rivers of water, that bringeth forth his fruit in his season; his leaf also shall not wither; ..'

Psalm 52:8 says:
'But I am like a green olive tree in the house of God:.'

Psalm 92:12 says:
'The righteous shall flourish like the palm tree: he shall grow like a cedar in Lebanon.'

Psalm 37:35 says:
'I have seen the wicked in great power, spreading himself like a green bay tree.'

Jude 12 says:
'..trees whose fruit withereth, without fruit, twice dead, plucked up by the roots;'

Read the references below and explain what the dangers of fruitlessness are.

- Matthew 3: 7 – 10
- John 15: 1, 2, 6

- Jude 12, 13
- Matthew 7: 15 – 20

Note:

The consequence of not bearing fruit is crystal clear in Isaiah Chapter 5:4 – 7. Let us read it again and see what God Himself says:

'What could have been done more to my vineyard, that I have not done in it? Wherefore, when I looked that it should bring forth grapes, brought it forth wild grapes? And now go to; ***I will tell you what I will do to my vineyard: I will take away the hedge thereof, and it shall be eaten up ; and break down the wall thereof, and it shall be trodden down: And I will lay it waste: it shall not be pruned , nor digged ; but there shall come up briers and thorns: I will also command the clouds that they rain no rain upon it.*** For the vineyard of the LORD of hosts is the house of Israel, and the men of Judah his pleasant plant: and he looked for judgment, but behold oppression; for righteousness, but behold a cry.'

5. In this parable, we are told that the owner came seeking fruit but found none. What does this tell us about God and what He looks for in His children?

6. The owner of the vineyard waited for three years before deciding to cut down the fig-tree. What does this tell us about God's nature? Please read Psalm 103: 8.

7. What does the question: 'why cumbereth it the ground' mean (Luke 13:7)? How does this relate to the average church goer today?

8. You will notice that although the owner gave another year of 'grace', the condition given for the survival of the fig-tree remained the same (it has to bear fruit). What does this tell us about the consistency of God and the need to put His mercy in perspective with His Justice? Please read Exodus 34: 6, 7.

Note:

Many preach the gospel of God as if He is eager and ever ready to destroy the wicked and unrepentant. No doubt, God is a God of justice and will never overlook iniquity, however, He is also slow to anger and is not willing that any man should perish as we are told in II Peter 3:9. God is longsuffering waiting for the sinner to realise the error of his or her ways and turn to Him before it is too late.

9. What is the main reason for Christ choosing the believer as expressed in John 15:16?

10. Who is the One that enables us to bear fruit? Please read John 15:5.

Note:

It is important to know that we cannot produce fruit without Christ. Wil Pounds explains: **'The command is not to produce fruit, but to abide. When we are abiding in Christ the fruit comes naturally. He produces it in us. If we abide in Christ we will bear fruit. If we don't, we become barren. The Vine is incomplete without the branches. He must have His branches to produce His fruit. When we abide He produces His fruit in us. We do not have to work at it. We don't have to agonize over it.**

We don't struggle to produce these characteristics of Christ. The Vin brings them about naturally. Good sweet grapes simply stay on the vin and let the life of the vine produce the fruit. Good spiritual fruit come naturally from God's vineyard.

When we abide in Christ, we are at the centre of God's will. It i impossible to abide in Christ and be outside of His will. When we abid in Him, He opens our spiritual eyes to see where He is working. H doesn't want us to bring to Him our great plans, and goals and decision and ask Him to bless them.

He wants us to seek His face and allow Him to guide us in doing wha He chooses for us to do. When our hearts are right with Him, He wi reveal to us where He is at work. We can dream up a lot of activities wit lots of green leaves and foliage, but no fruit of Spirit. "Apart from Me you can do nothing!"

Will we ever learn that truth? We can do many things; we can produce a lot of programs and religious activities, without depending on Christ We cannot produce His likeness unless we abide in Him.' Amen

LESSON 4

BEARING FRUIT

MAIN TEXT: JOHN 12: 23 – 25; 15: 1 – 5, 16 MATTHEW 7: 16 – 20

In the last lesson we observed that the owner of the vineyard threatened to cut down the fig tree because it bore no fruit. This brought to the fore an important question: 'What does it mean to bear fruit?'

Fruit bearing is commanded by the Lord and is indispensable. It is, therefore, important that we understand the Biblical definition of fruit bearing. To bear fruit simply means to be conformed into the image of Christ as a result of abiding in Him. God says: 'For whom he did foreknow, He also did predestinate to be conformed to the image of His Son, that He might be the firstborn among many brethren' (Romans 8:29).

The result of abiding in Christ will always lead to a Godly, holy and righteous life empowered by Christ Himself! Jesus categorically said that if we abide in Him we will bear fruit. This means that Christ is being reproduced in the life of each one of His disciples.

However, there is a need to consider this topic further and examine ourselves to see if we are bearing fruit in the light of Scripture.

1. What are some of the things that people mistake as evidence of fruit-bearing?

2. How does our fruit (and not our confession) define who we really are?
    - Matthew 7:16 –20
    - Titus 1: 16

Note:
Many continue to commit the very same sin that Cain committed. They consider their church attendance, water baptism, evangelism, tithes, offerings commitment to church activities as the major signs of bearing fruit. This is not the case! The Pharisees did the very same thing and yet they were condemned by Christ. Anything that originates from our own ability and all 'self-works' is unacceptable to God. It is an abomination to God. The scripture says: But we are all as an unclean thing, and all our righteousnesses are as filthy rags… (Isaiah 64:6).

Genuine fruit bearing is caused by the Spirit of God working in the believer and this will be evident as the very nature of Christ radiates through us.

3. One of the very first fruits we bear when we come to Christ is called 'the fruit of repentance'. How important is the fruit of repentance? Please refer to Matthew 3: 7 – 10.

4. As a result of abiding in Christ, the genuine Christian will mirror the fruit of the Spirit. Please read Galatians 5: 22, 23 and explain.

5. You will notice that the outworking of the Holy Spirit is called the 'fruit' of the Spirit and not the 'fruits' of the Spirit. Why do you think this is so and what is the implication?

Note:
It is very common to hear people say that they have some fruit of the Spirit but not the others. This is false doctrine. The fruit of the Spirit cannot be broken down into separate pieces. The fruit of the Spirit is one and pointing to one without the other is like trying to separate the colours of a rainbow. This is why it is called the fruit of the Spirit and not the fruits of the Spirit.

6. Romans 6:22 talks about another fruit called the fruit of holiness. What does this tell us about the relationship between the true Christian and holiness? Please use the references below to buttress your point:

- Romans 11: 16
- Romans 12: 1
- I Peter 1: 15, 16
- I Corinthians 3:16

7. Another fruit that the Bible refers to is the 'fruit of evangelism'. Please John 15: 16 and I Thessalonians 1: 6 – 8 and explain the meaning of the 'fruit of evangelism'.

8. In John 12:24 Jesus gave a condition on which we can bear fruit. What is it?

9. What does it mean to die as explained in verse 25 and 26 of John 12?

10. Explain Matthew 5: 13 – 16 in the light of fruit bearing.

Note:
J.C. Ryle admonishes:

Let us always remember, that baptism, church-membership, reception of the Lord's Supper, and a diligent use of the outward forms of Christianity, are not sufficient to save our souls.

They are leaves, nothing but leaves, and without fruit will add to our condemnation. Like the fig leaves of which Adam and Eve made themselves garments, they will not hide the nakedness of our souls from the eye of an all-seeing God, or give us boldness when we stand before Him at the last day. No! we must bear fruit, or be lost forever.

There must be fruit in our hearts and fruit in our lives, the fruit of repentance toward God, faith toward our Lord Jesus Christ, and true holiness in our conversation. Without such fruits as these a profession of Christianity will only sink us lower into hell.

LESSON 5

AN EXPOSITION OF ROMANS CHAPTER 6 (Part 1)
TEXT: Romans 6: 1 – 23

Romans Chapter 6 is an explicit exposition of the divine operation of God's grace in our lives. This Chapter is so central to the believer's faith that we cannot afford to approach its deep truths casually. Like all other Scripture, this wonderful Chapter requires nothing less than the Holy Spirit's interpretation in order to grasp the wonders of God's salvation and most importantly to enjoy the fullness of this blessed experience.

For those who prayerfully study it, the liberating power that emanates from God's word in this Chapter, is amazing and life-changing indeed! The book of Romans in general has been referred to by many as a masterpiece. Before Paul's exposition in Chapter 6, under the inspiration of the Holy Spirit, he systematically explains some of the fundamental tenets of the Christian faith, namely:

- God's holy wrath against all sin and its perpetrators (Chapter 1). This is summarised in Romans 1:32: '***Who knowing the judgement of God, that they which commit such things are worthy of death, not only do the same, but have pleasure in them that do them'.***

- The depravity and guilt of the entire world necessitates a 'common' salvation plan for all, both Jews and Gentiles alike (Chapter 2 and 3). This is summarised in Romans 3:9, 19 and 23: ***'What then? Are we better than they? No, in no wise: for we have before proved both Jews and Gentiles, that they are all under sin…Now we know that what things soever the law saith, it saith to them who are under the law: that every***

mouth may be stopped, and all the world may become guilty befo[re] God...For all have sinned, and come short of the glory of God...'

- The Jews and Gentiles are justified by faith through the death an[d] resurrection of our Lord and Saviour Jesus Christ (Chapter 3 and 4). Th[is] is summarised in Romans 3:24 – 26 and Romans 4:25: ***'being justifie[d] freely by His grace through the redemption that is in Christ Jesu[s]: Whom God hath set forth to be a propitiation through faith in H[is] blood, to declare His righteousness for the remission of sins that ar[e] past, through the forbearance of God; to declare, I say, at this tim[e] His righteousness: that He might be the just and the justifier of hi[m] which believeth in Jesus......Who (Jesus)was delivered for ou[r] offences, and was raised again for our justification'.***

- The entrance of sin into the world through one man called Adam thereb[y] leading to death and the entrance of the gift of righteousness that leads t[o] eternal life, given without the law, through One Man called Jesus Chris[t] (Chapter 5). This is summarised in Romans 5:12 – 17: ***'Wherefore, as b[y] one man sin entered into the world, and death by sin; and so deat[h] passed upon all men, for that all have sinned...for if by one man's offence death reigned by one; much more they which receiv[e] abundance of grace and of the gift of righteousness shall reign in lif[e] by One, Jesus Christ'.***

After Paul plainly points out in Chapters 1 – 5 that justification can only be attained by faith in the finished work of the cross and not by a laborious attempt to follow the law, he quickly moves on to explain that with the imputation of righteousness also comes the divinely imparted glorious life. He firmly underscores that imputation cannot be separated from impartation.

Many who have read Chapter 6 with reverence and total submission to God's word have testified of the liberating power received thereafter. May we all experience the same as we humbly study this lesson together - Amen.

1. Why did Paul ask the questions in Romans 6:1?

2. Paul answered his initial questions with another one in verse 2. Can you please explain the implication of what the Holy Spirit is saying here?

Note:

Paul knew that some were taking the doctrine of justification by grace for granted and were therefore emboldened in their life of sin. This is one of the oldest doctrinal errors that satan has injected into the church and which persists today. It is, therefore, no surprise that Paul vehemently opposes this doctrine of being saved in sin and continuing in sin.

This is the same false doctrine that Jude contended against and passionately denied: ***'For there are certain men crept in unawares, who were before of old ordained to this condemnation, ungodly men, turning the grace of our God unto lasciviousness, and denying the only Lord God, and our Lord Jesus Christ. I will therefore put you in remembrance, though ye once knew this, how that the Lord, having saved the people out of the land of Egypt, afterward destroyed them that believed not' (Jude 4,5).***

In Romans Chapter 6 verse 1, Paul uses very strong language to deny this damnable doctrine that states that one can be 'saved' and yet continue in sin. Apostle Peter in the same vein speaks vehemently against this doctrine in his second epistle.

'These are wells without water, clouds that are carried with a tempest to whom the mist of darkness is reserved for ever. For when they speak great swelling words of vanity, they allure through the lusts of the flesh through much wantonness, those that were clean escaped from them who live in error. While they promise them liberty, they themselves are the servants of corruption: for of whom a man is overcome, of the same is he brought in bondage.

***For if after they have escaped the pollutions of the world through the knowledge of the Lord and Saviour Jesus Christ, they are again entangled therein, and overcome, the latter end is worse with them than the beginning. For it had been better for them not to have known the way of righteousness, than, after they have known it, to turn from the holy commandment delivered unto them.'* (II Peter 2: 17 - 21).**

3. Please read Romans 6: 1 – 13 and state how many times Paul uses the word ***'dead', 'buried'*** *or* ***'crucified'***. What is God emphasising by using these words in describing the Christian experience?

4. Please explain the use of the word ***'dead', 'die' or 'crucified'*** in the following references and how does this relate to genuine Christian experience?

    - Colossians 3: 1 – 6
    - Galatians 5: 19 – 24
    - Galatians 2:20 and Galatians 6:14
    - Romans 8: 9 – 12
    - John 12: 24

5. Please read Romans 6: 3, 4 and explain what it means to be baptised into Jesus Christ's death?

6. You will notice that in Romans 6:3 – 5 and 8 – 11, ***'death'*** is always first spoken of before ***'life'.*** What is the Holy Spirit categorically telling the true church here?

Note:
It is futile to talk about the new life or being born again if the old life is not dead first. There is nowhere in Scripture where we are told that the old life will continue to be a drag on the believer after genuine conversion. Jesus Christ said expressly: ***'If the Son therefore shall make you free, ye shall be free indeed'*** (John 8:36). It is as simple and as plain as that! Therefore, if people in the church are not free indeed, God is not to be blamed!

Instead of seeking God until He rains righteousness upon us (Hosea 10:12), many relentlessly search for scriptures to defend their continuing entanglement with sin (a time-wasting effort and hopeless research designed to justify sinful living). There is a very great danger in wresting the scriptures for the purpose of defending error. II Peter 3:16 says: ***'.....which they that are unlearned and unstable wrest (the word), as they do also the other scriptures, unto their own destruction'.***

The widely used term 'born again', presupposes that something has first died before a second birth occurs. Do you remember the words of Jesus Christ when responding to the Pharisees? He said:

And he spake also a parable unto them; No man putteth a piece of a new garment upon an old; if otherwise, then both the new maketh a rent, and the piece that was taken out of the new agreeth not with the old. And no

man putteth new wine into old bottles; else the new wine will burst the bottles, and be spilled, and the bottles shall perish. But new wine must be put into new bottles; and both are preserved. (Luke 5: 36 – 38)

God will never mix the old with the new. It is either one or the other.

7. Many talk about a continuous and helpless struggle with the flesh and sin even after 'salvation'. How true is this in light of Romans 6:4?

8. You will notice in Romans 6: 4, 6, 8 the phrase 'with Him'. What is the spiritual meaning of this phrase?

9. Please read Romans 6:7, 18, 22 and explain what kind of freedom the Holy Spirit is speaking of here?

10. How does John 8:33 – 36 confirm the answer given to question 9 above?

11. God will not command us to do what is impossible. Can you explain what Romans 6: 12, 13 therefore implies?

12. Please read Romans 7: 14 – 21. Many have interpreted this passage of Scripture to mean that the believer will remain in a constant and embarrassing struggle with sin. How is this interpretation seriously at odds with Romans 6:12-14, 17-18, 22?

Jote:

'he truth is that people cannot experience what they do not believe. God ives grace to the humble. God clearly states: 'But now being made free :om sin, and become servants to God, ye have your fruit unto holiness, and ıe end everlasting life' (Romans 6: 22). Any experience short of this is not ;od's will and does not lead to eternal life.

LESSON 6

AN EXPOSITION OF ROMANS CHAPTER 6 (Part 2)
TEXT: Romans 6: 1 – 23

One of the key points highlighted in the previous lesson is the consistent us of the words ***'dead', 'crucified'*** and ***'buried'*** by the Apostle Paul to signi what happens to the 'old life' at the point of embracing the cross of Chris The cross of Christ is far more than a piece of emblem that people wear o their necks or hang on their walls. The cross of Christ is the very power of th living God and it is here that we are invited to bring the 'old man' for executior This is why Paul declares in I Corinthians 1:18 that the preaching of the cros ***'is the power of God.'***

In the days of the old Roman Empire, whenever a new cross was bein prepared everyone knew for certain that another life would soon be gone. N one survived the cross as the cross had no mercy. It was a 'one-way ticket' fo those who were led to the cross for crucifixion as no one ever came back alive The cross gave no clemency neither did it have any pity on its victim. The cros meant an execution of a life.

The believers in Rome, who had witnessed so many executions in their time understood the message of Paul. Just as the physical cross had power to execut its victim, so also, the cross of Christ has the power to crucify the 'old-man'. I the old-man has been taken to the cross for execution, it would no longer hav dominion over the believer. This is the central teaching of Scripture. What a glorious message! A glorious experience awaits all who simply believe God's word.

We were never meant to live our spiritual lives side-by-side with the old-man alive and kicking from within. It is an aberration and a denial of God's truth to believe such damnable heresy and to preach the same. Galatians 5:24 says:

'they that are Christ's have crucified the flesh with the affections and lusts.' Praise the Lord - we are crucified with Christ!

You will notice how the Holy Spirit inspires Paul to set out very clear distinctions between the saved and the unsaved. There is an undeniable dichotomy that runs through Romans Chapter

Some of which are as follows:

- 'Instruments of unrighteousness unto sin' versus 'instruments of righteousness unto God' – Romans 6:13
- 'Dead to sin' versus 'Alive unto God' – Romans 6:11
- 'Sin unto death' versus 'Obedience unto righteousness'– Romans 6:16
- 'Servants of sin' versus 'Servants of righteousness' – Romans 6:17, 18
- 'Free from righteousness' versus 'Free from sin' – Romans 6:20, 18
- 'Yield your members servants to uncleanness and to iniquity unto iniquity' versus 'Yield your members servants to righteousness unto holiness' – Romans 6:19

May the breath of the Holy Spirit give us understanding and divine enablement to walk in the light of His holy word.

1. How is the believer portrayed in Romans 6:11 -15? Is it as a victor over the power of sin or as a slave to sin?

2. Please read verse 14 and explain the relationship betwcen grace and power over sin.

Note:

True grace never leaves the sincere seeker powerless, timid and in bondage to sin. Such an experience is not consistent with the operation of the grace of God in the believer's life. True grace is the embodiment of God's power. True grace dislodges, dismantles and destroys the yoke of sin. True grace has the power to slay our former ***'sin-master'*** called the old-man. True grace cuts the chains of iniquity that once held us captive. Sin no longer has dominion over the believer.

This is not because we struggle against sin and eventually succeed as some erroneously preach, but because of the almighty work of God's abounding grace in our lives. If we are unsure of what God has promised us we would not know what to pray for and if we do not pray for the right experience, we obviously will not live it.

We are not called to 'grow' out of sin as believers. If this were possible Paul would not have cried out in frustration, ***'Oh wretched man that I am!'*** (Romans 7:24) when as an unbeliever, he experienced the futility of trying to grow out of sin.

The definition of true grace is given by God in Titus 2: 11 – 14:

'For the grace of God that bringeth salvation hath appeared to all men, Teaching us that, denying ungodliness and worldly lusts, we should live soberly, righteously, and godly, in this present world; Looking for that blessed hope, and the glorious appearing of the great God and our Saviour Jesus Christ; Who gave himself for us, that he might redeem us from all iniquity, and purify unto himself a peculiar people, zealous of good works'.

3. What does Paul mean when he says we are not under the law in Romans 6:14?

4. The test of true grace is obedience. Can you please explain?

Note:

True grace empowers the believer to obey the Lord. To profess that we are recipients of God's grace and find ourselves incapable of obeying God's word is a travesty of the gospel. As pointed out in the references below, you will notice how God places emphasis on obedience in the current dispensation of grace.

- **Romans 2:8** – 'But unto them that are contentious, and do not ***obey the truth***, but obey unrighteousness, indignation and wrath'
- **Romans 6: 17** – '...but you ***have obeyed from the heart that form of doctrine***...'
- **Galatians 3:1** – '...who hath bewitched you that you should not ***obey the truth***,..'
- **II Thessalonians 3:14** – '..And if any man ***obey not our word by this epistle***, note that man, and have no company with him, that he may be ashamed'.
- **Romans 6:16** – '…to whom you yield yourselves ***servants to obey, his servants ye are to whom ye obey***...'
- **I Peter 4:17** – 'For the time is come that judgement must begin at the house of God: and if it first begin at us, what shall the end be of them ***that obey not the gospel of God?***

5. How important is obedience under the dispensation of grace?

6. What is the relationship between Paul's statement in Romans 6:16: ***'...his servants ye are to whom ye obey'*** and the words of Jesus Christ in John 8:34: ***'Verily, verily I say unto you, Whosoever committeth sin is the servant of sin.'***?

7. Taking into consideration the answers you have just given to question 6, please read I John 3:8. What conclusions do you draw on how God views anyone still under the power of sin despite their confession of Christ?

Note:
God's judgement is always against the 'actions' of sin irrespective of the perpetrator. God does not see sin on the basis of whether we 'confess' Christ or not. The anger of an unbeliever is no different from the one who professes to know Christ even though he or she might claim to have responded to an altar call some time ago. This is why, even under the dispensation of grace, God warns against sin:

Galatians 5: 19 -21

'Now the works of the flesh are manifest, which are these; Adultery, fornication, uncleanness, lasciviousness, Idolatry, witchcraft, hatred, variance, emulations, wrath, strife, seditions, heresies, Envyings, murders, drunkenness, revellings, and such like: of the which I tell you before, as I have also told you in time past, that they which do such things shall not inherit the kingdom of God'.

Corinthians 6: 9 – 11

Know ye not that the unrighteous shall not inherit the kingdom of God? Be not deceived: neither fornicators, nor idolaters, nor adulterers, nor ffeminate, nor abusers of themselves with mankind, Nor thieves, nor ovetous, nor drunkards, nor revilers, nor extortioners, shall inherit the ingdom of God'.

Revelation 21:8

But the fearful, and unbelieving, and the abominable, and murderers, and whoremongers, and sorcerers, and idolaters, and all liars, shall have heir part in the lake which burneth with fire and brimstone: which is he second death.

8. What is the significance of Paul using the phrase 'ye were….' in Romans 6: 17, 20?

9. Can you identify other Scripture references where the past tense is used to denote the passing away of the old-life?

10. It is very clear from our text that we cannot be both servant of sin and righteousness at the same time. Does this contradict Galatians 5:17? Please give reason(s) for your answer.

11. At the end of Romans Chapter 6 Paul says: '…the wages of sin is death' Since we know that he was not referring to the world outside but 'church people', what is the implication of this statement to the sinning professors of Christianity?

12. If we take Romans Chapter 6 to the Lord in fervent prayer and meticulously pray each verse into our lives what do you think will happen?

Note:

Let us not be hearers of the word only. Pray this chapter into your life until th chains of sin and the bondage of iniquity is broken from your life. Read ever verse to yourself in the presence of the Almighty God. Hold onto the horns c the altar until the witness of the Spirit confirms that it is done. Do not bothe about what others preach or believe. Every man will give account of himse before God. The word of God is effectual and is more than able to crucify th old-man.

Take the old-man to the cross for execution! Pray that God will nail your 'old man' to the cross. Pray for the 'old-man' to be executed, dead and burie according to the word of God. Pray that the glory of God will give you th power to walk in the newness of life for sin shall no longer have dominion ove you.

The question is not whether this is possible, the real question is if you desir this promised experience more than anything else. Those who hunger anc thirst for righteousness will truly be filled. Our eternity depends on it!

LESSON 7

AN EXPOSITION OF ROMANS CHAPTER 7 (Part 1)
TEXT: Romans 7: 1 – 8

In Romans Chapter 6, Paul the apostle primarily addresses the issue of the believer's relationship to sin. The core message of the Chapter is summarised in verses 6 and 14: ***'Knowing this, that our old man is crucified with him, that the body of sin might be destroyed, that henceforth we should not serve sin. For sin shall not have dominion over you: for ye are not under the law, but under grace.'***

Having addressed the subject of the believer's relationship to sin in the previous Chapter, Paul moves on to address the subject of the believer's relationship to the law in Chapter 7. An antithesis exists between Romans Chapters 6 and 7. In Romans Chapter 6, the key word is **'sin'** and it appears seventeen times in the Chapter. The key word in Chapter 7 is ***'law'*** and it is used twenty-three times in the Chapter.

Whilst Chapter 6 explains the believer's ***relationship to sin,*** in Romans Chapter 7 we see the believer's ***relationship to the law***. While Romans 6:14 emphasises the believer's freedom from the ***dominion of sin***, Romans 7:1, 2 emphasises the believer's freedom from the ***dominion of the law***. The believer is ***dead to sin*** in Romans 6:2 while he is ***dead to the law*** in Romans 7:4. In Romans 6:18 we are told that the believer is ***free from sin*** and in Romans 7:3, 6 the believer is said to be ***free from the law***. The believer walks ***in the newness of life*** according to Romans 6:4 and in Romans 7:6 we are told to serve in ***newness of spirit.***

Another key word used in Romans Chapter 7 is ***'I'***. This word is used over thirty times. Its frequent use is to point out that any attempt to observe the law in our own strength will never lead to a victorious life over sin. Consequently, while Romans Chapter 6 speaks of our victory in ***'Christ'***, Romans Chapter 7 highlights our defeat in self-reliance called ***'I'***.

1. Please explain the different emphasis in Romans Chapters 6 and 7.

Note:

Paul starts Chapter 7 by using a phrase that he often uses in his epistles. It is the phrase ***'Know ye not'***. Whenever Paul uses this phrase he is invariably saying that his audience should not be ignorant about a particular truth or that they should know better. Some examples are as follows:

- *Know ye not*, that so many of us as were baptized into Jesus Christ were baptized into his death? (Romans 6:3)
- *Know ye not,* that to whom ye yield yourselves servants to obey, his servants ye are to whom ye obey; (Romans 6:16)
- Know ye not brethren, (for I speak to them that know the law,) how that the law hath dominion over a man as long as he liveth? (Romans 7:1)
- *Know ye not* that ye are the temple of God, and that the Spirit of God dwelleth in you? (I Corinthians 3: 16)
- Your glorying is not good. *Know ye not* that a little leaven leaveneth the whole lump? (I Corinthians 5:6)
- *Know ye not* that we shall judge angels? how much more things that pertain to this life? (I Corinthians 6:3)
- *Know ye not* that the unrighteous shall not inherit the kingdom of God? (I Corinthians 6:9)

- *Know ye not* that your bodies are the members of Christ? shall I then take the members of Christ, and make them the members of an harlot? God forbid. (I Corinthians 6: 15)

- What? *know ye not* that he which is joined to an harlot is one body? for two, saith he, shall be one flesh. (I Corinthians 6:16)

- What? *know ye not* that your body is the temple of the Holy Ghost which is in you, which ye have of God, and ye are not your own? (I Corinthians 6:19)

- *Know ye not* that they which run in a race run all, but one receiveth the prize? So run, that ye may obtain (I Corinthians 9:24).

- Examine yourselves, whether ye be in the faith; prove your own selves. *Know ye not* your own selves, how that Jesus Christ is in you, except ye be reprobates? (II Corinthians 13:5)

2. Please examine each of the above '***Know ye not***' statements and explain what each statement means and its implication.

3. Please read Romans 7:1–4. Paul once again underscores the indispensability of dying to the 'old life' in order to live the 'new life'. Please relate these verses to what has been earlier said in Romans Chapter 6.

4. Paul uses the sacredness of the marriage covenant to explain his message. What truth(s) do we learn about the ***'marriage covenant'*** from these verses?

5. Towards the end of Romans 7:4, Paul affirms that being dead to the law will lead to bringing ***'forth fruit unto God'.*** How does this confirm an earlier statement made in Romans 3:31?

6. Can you please explain what Romans 7:5 means?

Note:

Verse 5 brings us to a very important juncture in Romans Chapter 7 and summarises what Paul says in verses 6 – 25. This serves as a preface to the ensuing description that Paul gives with regards to the relationship between the flesh (the old-man), the law and sin. From this point onward, Paul emphasises that without the crucifixion of the old-man, any attempt to fulfil the demands of the law will be futile, frustrating and will lead to spiritual death! In the latter part of verse 5, Paul states that such an attempt will only ***'bring forth fruit unto death.'***

Unfortunately, many fail to link the rest of the Chapter with verse 5 and erroneously say (in reference to Romans 7:14) that even after Paul's 'conversion', he was still carnal and struggled with sin. We should, however, notice that the beginning of verse 5 starts with the words: ***'For when we were in the flesh…'.*** Paul's usage of the past tense here denotes that the events that he is about to illustrate refers to his past life.

For this reason, just before Paul describes his former life of frustration with the flesh and with sin, he reminds the brethren in verse 6: ***'But now we are delivered from the law, that being dead wherein we were held; that we should serve in newness of spirit, and not in the oldness of the letter'.***

Please read Romans 7: 6. What do the following phrases denote in relation to genuine salvation?

- **'But now...'**
- **'being dead wherein we were held…'**
- **'serve in newness of spirit…'**

. The phrase **'but now…'** in verse 6 is also used by Paul in other Scriptures. Please read the following references and discuss the implication of this phrase in each text.

- Romans 3: 21
- Romans 6:22
- Romans 7: 6
- Ephesians 2: 13
- Ephesians 5:8
- Colossians 3:8

9. In Romans 7:7 Paul asked the question: **'Is the law sin?'** Why do you think he asked this question?

Note:

Although Paul says in verse 4 that we are dead to the law, he did not want tl brethren to think that there was anything wrong with the law itself. The la has never been the problem! Rather, the problem has always been wit mankind. Man's incapacity, before conversion, to obey the law due to his falle nature has always been the problem. Paul wanted to make it very clear that th law was not man's stumbling block. This is why he asks the question ***'is th law sin?'***

The central theme of Paul's epistle to the Romans was to point out the futilit of trying to develop a relationship with God on the basis of an outwar adherence to the law. Paul, therefore, focuses much on this subject and nc surprisingly mentions the word ***'law' over*** **'70'** times in the Book of Roman (23 times in Chapter 7 alone).

In the earlier Chapters (Chapters 1 – 5), Paul consistently points out that n one has the power to obey the law in his or her own strength. Yet in the sam vein, he does not want to leave any room for us to misconstrue his messag and think that the problem is with the law. Consequently, Paul makes a ver stern defence of the law in Romans 7:12: ***'Wherefore the law is holy, and th commandment holy, and just, and good'.***

Furthermore in Romans 8:3 Paul says: ***'For what the law could not do, <u>IN THAT IT WAS WEAK THROUGH THE FLESH,</u> God sending hi own Son in the likeness of sinful flesh, and for sin, CONDEMNED SIN IN THE FLESH:'***

You will notice from the above text that God does not lay the problem at the 'feet' of the law but the flesh! It was the flesh that was weak. This is why it says sin was condemned in the flesh and not in the law.

10. Please read the following texts and have a general discussion about what each reference tells us about the law.

- Galatians 3: 21
- Galatians 3:24
- I Timothy 1: 8 - 10
- Romans 3:20
- Romans 3: 31

11. Please read Romans 7: 7-8 and explain what Paul is saying here.

Note:
The law is good. The law is just. The law is holy. The epistle of James says that all good and perfect gifts come from God and since God gave the law, He definitely gave us something good. The Gospel according to Matthew 7:11 confirms that if we on earth, being evil, know how to give good gifts to our children how much more our Father in heaven.

A very common statement we hear today is that ***'we are no longer under the law'.*** It is true that our relationship with God is not based on a mere outward adherence to the law. However, it is equally true that after we come into a true relationship with God through Jesus Christ, God demands that the moral standard of the law be upheld. God has not changed.

What did God say about the New Covenant?

'For this is the covenant that I will make with the house of Israel after those days, saith the Lord; I WILL PUT MY LAWS INTO THEIR MIND, and write them in their hearts: and I will be to them a God, and they shall be to me people.' - Hebrews 8:10

The New Covenant established by God does not abandon the moral law. Th truth is that in the New Covenant, God puts His law in our hearts. The Ne Covenant has nothing to do with living the way we like.

Do you know why God places His law in our hearts? It is because we are tol in Proverbs 23:7 that: ***'For as he thinketh in his HEART so is he.'*** We ca only live-out what is inside of us.

Show me someone who kicks against the law of God under the guise of bein in the New Covenant and I will show you someone who has no tru relationship with the God of the New Covenant.

LESSON 8

AN EXPOSITION OF ROMANS CHAPTER 7 (Part 2)
TEXT: Romans 7: 9 - 25

We learnt in the previous lesson that there is nothing wrong with the law. Just as Paul points out the gross limitations of trying to develop a fruit-bearing relationship with God on the basis of the law, in the same vein, he is careful not to give the slightest impression that the law itself is the 'villain' hindering us from serving God. In Romans 7:10 Paul says that the ***commandment was ordained by God for life***.

There are several Scriptures that speak about the goodness of the law and these support Paul's teaching in Romans. Jesus Christ said: **'Think not that I am come to destroy the law, or the prophets: I am not come to destroy, but to fulfil'.** (Matthew 5:17). When the rich young ruler asked Jesus Christ what to do in order to inherit eternal life, Jesus pointed him to the law (Luke 10:25 – 28).

In Luke 16:17 Jesus Christ said: ***'And it is easier for heaven and earth to pass, than one tittle of the law to fail'.*** Romans 2:15 talks about the ***'work of the law'*** written in the hearts of the Gentiles who were never part of the commonwealth of Israel. The Psalmist speaks in defence of the law by saying that the ***'The law of the Lord is perfect***, converting the soul.' (Psalm 19:7).

In Hebrews 8:7-9 we are categorically told that the fault experienced in the first covenant has nothing to do with the law but with the people:

'For if that first covenant had been faultless, then should no place have been sought for the second. *For finding fault with them* (not the law), he saith, Behold, the days come, saith the Lord, when I will make a new covenant with the house of Israel and with the house of Judah: Not according to the covenant that I made with their fathers in the day when I took them by the hand to lead them out of the land of Egypt; *because*

***they continued not in my covenant*, and I regarded them not, saith the Lord'.**

You will notice that in Romans 7:4 we are not told that the law is dead, but rather, we are dead to the law. It says: ***'Wherefore, my brethren, ye also are become dead to the law by the body of Christ…'*** This is repeated in Galatians 2:19, where Paul says that he is the one who is dead to the law and not the other way round.

The truth that Paul emphasises in Romans 7 is this, although the law is good, holy and just, it was never intended to give spiritual life to the believer. Paul points out that sinful flesh is too weak and vulnerable to fulfil the demands of the good and holy law. Paul then gives an illustration of his own experience as an unbeliever. He describes how he found himself totally incapacitated by the flesh and the dominating power of sin and therefore ended up being unable to obey the very law he desperately pursued.

1. Why is it so important for Paul to point out that there is nothing wrong with the law?

2. Though good, holy and just what was the limitation of the law?

Note:
The law serves as an 'excellent mirror' showing how sinful mankind is but does not go any further. It does not provide a remedy for man's sin. The law is firm, uncompromising and strict! The law declares the demands of our Holy God. The law examines every minute detail of our life in light of God's holy standard but does not provide the power required to meet those demands. It is, however, not the fault of the law that man is sinful.

God uses the law to amplify (not exaggerate) man's sins so that he can clearly see the true state of his heart in light of God's word. It is only those who understand the exceeding righteousness of God's law that will understand the exceeding sinfulness of man's nature before conversion (please read Romans :13).

The law reveals man's iniquitous state but does not have the 'power' to provide the solution. Galatian 3:21 underscores both the goodness, as well as, the limitation of the law. **'Is the law then against the promises of God? God forbid: for if there had been a law given which could have given life, verily righteousness should have been by the law'.**

Those who run to the law for the solution miss the point regarding the purpose of the law. Many find their hopes dashed as they come to the painful reality that the law cannot produce in them the righteous life demanded by God. What are we to do when we realise that the law, though good, cannot provide a remedy for our sinful nature?

The Scripture tells us that, the realisation of the law's inability to deliver us from sin is what leads the sincere seeker wholeheartedly to Christ. Hence, the law is the 'agent' that God uses to show our desperate need for Christ. In Galatians 3:24 we are told: ***'Wherefore the law was our schoolmaster to bring us unto Christ, that we might be justified by faith.'*** As we experience the limitation of the law, we come to the knowledge that only Christ can deliver us from the power of sin and it is only through Him (and not the law), that we can live the holy life demanded by our Holy God.

It is also noteworthy to mention that even in The Old Testament, God never intended the Israelites to seek remedy from the law. Habakkuk, an Old Testament prophet, said the just shall live by FAITH (and not by the law!) – Habakkuk 2:4.

Paul reiterates in Galatians 2:16:

'Knowing that a man is not justified by the works of the law, but by the fai of Jesus Christ, even we have believed in Jesus Christ, that we might be justifie by the faith of Christ, and not by the works of the law: for by the works of th law shall no flesh be justified'.

3. Please read the following texts and explain the purpose of the law.
   - Galatians 3:19
   - Galatians 3:24

4. Paul identifies sin as the 'real culprit' and stumbling block to man' relationship with God (and not the law). Please refer to Romans 7: 8, 11 13 and explain the meaning of these verses.

Note:

The law does not bring death, it is SIN that brings DEATH:

'For the wages of sin is death; but the gift of God is eternal life throug Jesus Christ our Lord' (Romans 6:23).

'Was then that which is good (the law) made death unto me? God forbid But sin, that it might appear sin, working death in me by that which i good; that sin by the commandment might become exceeding sinful' (Romans 7:13)

'For I was alive without the law once: but when the commandment came, <u>sin revived, and I died'</u> (Romans 7:9).

'Then when lust hath conceived, it bringeth forth sin: and sin, when it is finished, <u>bringeth forth death'</u> (James 1: 15).

5. Please read Romans 7:14 and explain why 'the spiritual law' and 'the carnal man' cannot work together.

6. Many assume that Paul was still under the power of sin even after his conversion. Romans 7:14 is the Scripture normally used to justify their position. Can you please point out verses in Romans 6 that negate such assertion?

Note:
Reference to Paul's own experience in Romans Chapter 7 has to do with his incapacity to serve the Lord as an unconverted Pharisee and not as a saved soul (as some erroneously claim). Paul's illustration starts with an introductory statement given in verse 5: ***'For when we were in the flesh (past tense), the motions of sins, which were by the law, did work in our members to bring forth fruit unto death.'***

It is on the basis of verse 5 that Paul gives a vivid picture of his own painful frustration of trying to develop a relationship with God through the law. To say that Paul was struggling with sin as an Apostle not only negates the whole message in Romans Chapter 6, but automatically disqualifies him from being an apostle.

Romans 7:14 – 25 is not the only time when Paul uses the present tense to illustrate an experience of the past. In Timothy 1:15 Paul says: ***'This is a faithful saying, and worthy of all acceptation, that Christ Jesus came into the world to save sinners; of whom I am chief.'*** Is Paul saying that he was still a 'practising' chief sinner as at the time of writing?

No, certainly not, for he says later on in Galatians 2:17: ***'But if, while we seek to be justified by Christ, we ourselves also are found sinners, is therefore Christ the minister of sin? God forbid.'*** It is always good to compare Scripture with Scripture in order to arrive at true and informed biblical conclusions.

7. Please compare Romans 7:14 with I Thessalonians 2:10. Does this look like the testimony of the same 'saved' person?

Note:
On one hand Paul says that he is **'carnal'** and **'sold under sin'** (Romans 7:14) and the next moment we see him testify of how he behaved himself **'holily'**, **'justly'** and **'unblameably'** amongst the believers at Thessalonica. Definitely, Paul could not have been living both lives concurrently. What Paul depicted in Romans Chapter 7: 14 - 25 referred to his past life.

Do you know that Paul wrote to the brethren at Thessalonica before writing to the brethren at Rome? Therefore, if we say that what Paul wrote in Romans Chapter 7 related to his present life, then it invariably means that, as at the time of writing the epistle, Paul had 'backslidden' from the holy life earlier testified of in I Thessalonians 2:10

Before his conversion, Paul admits: ***'Now then it is no more I that do it, but sin that dwelleth in me' (Romans 7:17), but after his conversion we hear***

him say in Galatians 2:20: 'I am crucified with Christ nevertheless I live: yet not I but Christ liveth in me…'

Consequently, prior to salvation, Paul says it is not I but sin that dwells in me and after salvation he says it is not I but Christ who dwells in me. Before salvation we are conquered by 'sin' but after salvation we are conquered by God's love leading to obedience. Praise the Lord!

8. Are we meant to be slaves to the power of sin after salvation? Please refer to the following references for your answer.

    - John 8: 34 – 36
    - Romans 6: 18
    - I John 3:8, 9
    - Luke 1: 74,75

9. Please read Romans 7: 14 – 20, 23. Does this give the picture of a victor or a slave?

10. What does genuine salvation do in the life of the believer? Please refer to the following Scriptures for your answer.

    - Titus 2: 11, 12
    - Ephesians 1:4
    - Romans 8: 10 - 13

11. What does Paul's question in Romans 7:24 reveal to us about the focus of the true salvation message?

12. II Timothy 3: 5 shows us how God views any kind of 'salvation' that lacks power to deliver from sin. Can you please explain?

Note:

Paul introduces Jesus Christ (in Romans 7:25) as the only answer to conquering the flesh and the power of sin. The law is meant to lead us to Christ and this is what the message of Romans 7 is about. Our incapacity to keep God's holy law in our own strength should lead us to the Saviour. The frustration of fighting and failing is meant to bring the sincere seeker face-to-face with Christ for total and permanent deliverance.

Have you truly experienced the triumphant power of Christ in your life? If you have, you will no longer be struggling with sin. You will not be rising and falling if the Greater One is in you. This is the time to pray and obtain the victory provided at the cross. This is the time to approach the Throne of Grace for the glorious victory spoken about in Romans Chapter 8.

LESSON 9

AN EXPOSITION OF ROMANS CHAPTER 8
TEXT: Romans 8: 1 – 14

efore examining today's lesson in detail, it is noteworthy to point out that the eginning of Romans Chapter 8 is a direct response to Paul's lamentation in omans 7:24: ***'O wretched man that I am! Who shall deliver me from the ody this of death?'*** Jesus Christ is the answer to that question. Jesus Christ ame to save us from the body of death called the old-man or the sinful nature. n Romans 7:25 Paul points to Jesus Christ as the deliverer from the body of eath.

'he Lord did not come to save us in sin but to save us from sin and this is why he Gospel of Christ emphasises our deliverance from the 'body of death' all hrough Scripture. In Romans 6:6 we are told: 'Knowing this, that our old man s crucified with him, ***that the body of sin might be destroyed***, that ienceforth we should not serve sin'.

Ve have the same truth reiterated in Romans 8:10: **And if Christ be in you, *he body is dead because of sin*; but the Spirit is life because of ighteousness'**. Another statement of truth in relation to the believer's leliverance from the body of death can be found in Colossians 2:11 which says: ***…ye are circumcised with the circumcision made without hands, in outting off the body of the sins of the flesh by the circumcision of Christ:'***

1. If you were to respond to Paul's question, ***'Who shall deliver me from this body of death?'*** what would your answer be?

Note:

In Chapter 8, Paul shifts his focus from man's inherent weakness in the flesh, as exposed by the law, and now emphasises the believer's victory through the

Holy Spirit. You will notice a very simple yet important word in Romans 8: It is the word 'now'.

'There is therefore NOW no condemnation to them which are in Christ Jesu who walk not after the flesh, but after the Spirit.' Romans 8:1

The word 'now', as used by Paul in verse 1, puts an undisputable finality to th slavish sinful-life described in the previous chapter. It implies that the believe at salvation moves from this life of sinful bondage into a victorious life i Christ, enabled and empowered by the Holy Spirit. This verse can be bette understood as explained below:

Important word or phrase	**Explanation**
'Now'	'Now' refers to the present. It means something old ceases to exist. Paul having painted a gloomy picture of the enslaved life in Romans 7, and rightly so, now points out that the believer has been brought to the threshold of a new experience. The word 'now' has a dual purpose. It terminates the past slavish sinful life and ushers us into the beautiful fragrance of the new life found in Christ Jesus.
'in Christ Jesus'	This phrase summarises everything about the Christian faith. Our faith is not based on outward rituals, it is about being in Christ. Our calling is a call to come into Christ. Our victory is assured if we are truly in Christ. The flesh no longer has dominion over those who are in Christ. Only those who are in Christ can walk in the newness of life.
'who walk not after the flesh, but after the Spirit'	This is the real evidence of being in Christ. Those in Christ walk after the Spirit. They mind the things of the Spirit. They are empowered by the Spirit and experience victory by the Spirit.

2. Who are those in Christ Jesus according to Romans 8:1?

3. What is the consequence of walking in the flesh? Please refer to the following references for your answer.

    - Romans 8: 6 – 8
    - Romans 8: 12, 13
    - Galatians 6:8
    - II Peter 2: 9, 10, 18 – 20

4. Paul in the previous chapter gives an elaborate explanation of not being under the power of the law, but in Romans 8:2 he now talks about 'the law of the Spirit'. What does this mean?

Note:
The fact that believers are not to establish their relationship with God on the basis of the law does not mean that we become lawless or indifferent to the law of God. Many might be surprised to know that the believer's life is moulded and empowered by the Holy Spirit to fulfil the demands of the law. The New Testament era does not discard the moral standard of the law. In Romans 8:3, 4 we are told that the essence of grace is that the righteousness of the law might be fulfilled in us:

For what the law could not do, in that it was weak through the flesh, <u>God sending his own Son in</u> the likeness of sinful flesh, and for sin, condemned sin in the flesh: That <u>the righteousness of the law might be fulfilled in us</u>, who walk not after the flesh, but after the Spirit.

It is therefore not surprising to find the word 'law' used in the New Testament Apart from 'the law of the Spirit' (Romans 8:2), other use of the word 'law' ir the New Testament include;

- The Law of Christ – Galatians 6:2
- The Law of Faith – Romans 3: 27
- The Law of Liberty – James 1: 25
- The Law of Righteousness – Romans 9:31

5. There is a statement in Romans 8:3 that beautifully describes the grace of God. What do you think that statement is?

Note:
The Christian faith is not founded on what we can do for God but on what He has done for us and what He continues to do. Simply put, this is called 'grace'. We are told that God sent His Son in the likeness of sinful flesh in order to condemn sin and set us free from the yoke of the flesh. (Romans 8:3).

This is what makes the Christian faith different from the religions of the world. While religion tells us to do something in order to appease God and get His favour, the Christian faith shares the good news of what God has done for us and what He continues to do in us. The message of the Christian faith is salvation by grace. However, the only message religion can offer, is 'salvation by works'. Religion is man's attempt to reach God. The Christian faith is God's love reaching out to man.

The Jews must have been surprised at the response received from Jesus Christ when they asked Him: ***'What shall we do, that we might work the works of God?*** (John 6:28). This was purely a religious question. It was a question that emphasised on man doing something in order to appease God. It was a question that reflected their misplaced theology that we must do something in our strength in order to reach God. Jesus Christ replied: ***This is the work of God, that you believe on Him (Jesus) whom He (God) hath sent'.*** (John 6:29). This summarises the Christian faith and Christ's answer must have shocked the religious people of His days.

It is this blessed truth that Paul alludes to when he reminds the church in Romans 8:3 that God sent His Son for the purpose of addressing sin and man's inherent carnal nature. Thank God for the gospel of grace! Thank God we are not called to religion!

6. Please read the following references and explain how each reflects the grace of God.

    - Romans 5:6 – 8
    - Philippians 1:6
    - Philippians 2:13
    - I Thessalonians 3:12,13
    - Colossians 1: 12, 13
    - Philippians 4:19
    - Titus 3: 4 - 6

7. Please give other scriptures, similar to the ones given in question (6) above, that highlight the 'gospel of grace'.

8. Please compare Romans 8:5 with John 3: 6 and explain the similarity.

9. Please read the following references and explain how God describes the carnal person?

   - Romans 7: 14,15
   - I Corinthians 3: 1 – 5

10. Please refer to what Paul wrote in Romans 8: 6 – 8 and explain what the consequences of being carnally-minded are.

Note:
Paul gives very clear illustrations about the contrast existing between the flesh and the Spirit. He highlights in Romans 8: 1 – 14 that the difference between the Spirit and the flesh is so undeniably clear. Salvation is not a muddled-up experience that lacks distinction. It is for this reason that Paul repetitively, and deliberately too, mentions the flesh side-by-side the Spirit. This he does so as to make it crystal clear that there is an irreconcilable dichotomy between the flesh and the Spirit.

You will notice some of the contrast highlighted below:

Verse	Flesh	Spirit
verses 3, 4	The flesh is weak and has no power to fulfil the demands of the law.	The Spirit succeeds where the flesh fails by enabling the believer to fulfil the demands of the law.
verse 5	The flesh incapacitates the unbeliever from being spiritually minded.	The Spirit enables the believer to be spiritually minded.
verse 6	The flesh leads to death	The Spirit leads to life and peace.
verse 9	The one in the flesh does not belong to Christ	The one in the Spirit belongs to Christ
verse 10	The flesh makes the body alive to the power of sin	The Spirit crucifies the body to the dominating power of sin.

11. What evidence is given by Scripture to confirm that one has the in-dwelling Christ? Please read Romans 8:10 to support your answer.

12. How does Romans 8:11 once again reflect the grace of God?

Note:

The word 'Spirit' is used more than 10 times in Romans 8:1 – 14 and on eac occasion, it is with a capital 'S'. This again underscores the message of grac that it is God working in us and through us (which is the defining message (salvation). In Romans 8:11 we are told that ***if the Spirit of him that raise up Jesus from the dead dwell in you, he that raised up Christ from th dead shall also quicken your mortal bodies by his Spirit that dwelleth r you.***

Since the word 'Spirit' begins with a capital letter, it means that the above vers can be re-phrased to read as follows: ***If God that raised up Jesus from th dead dwells in you, God who raised up Jesus from the dead shall quicke your mortal bodies by God who dwells in you.***

The re-phrased statement shows that God and God alone is the one who work out our salvation. Thank God for the 'Gospel of Grace!'

LESSON 10

THE PARABLE OF THE SHEEP AND THE GOATS
TEXT: Matthew 25:31 - 46

One of the remarkable things about the parable of the sheep and the goats is the hidden undertone of Christ's message. Many have made the grave mistake of taking a casual approach to this parable and have therefore misinterpreted the whole message. It is very common for this parable to be interpreted as underlining the importance of helping the poor and showing compassion to the needy in the world.

Such interpretation is not only presumptuous but it also relegates the entire message to an exhortation to engage in secular acts of compassion. Such an interpretation is erroneous and in every way non-spiritual.

It is important, at this juncture, to remember that the carnal mind cannot understand the things of God no matter how 'simple' they seem to be on the surface. What the Bible says in I Corinthians 2:14 is noteworthy: **'But the natural man receiveth not the things of the Spirit of God: for they are foolishness unto him: neither can he know them, because they are spiritually discerned'**

It is equally important to reiterate that all of Jesus' parables, including this one, are essentially about God's kingdom. Hence the parable of the sheep and the goats is not a mere injunction to engage in good deeds from a humanitarian perspective.

'And the disciples came, and said unto Him' why speak thou unto them in parables? He answered and said unto them, because it is given unto you to know the **mysteries of the kingdom of heaven**, but to them it is not given' (Matthew 13: 10, 11).

With the above in mind, let us carefully and spiritually examine the parable o the sheep and the goats together.

Questions:

1. Read Matthew 25: 31 – 33. What does the fact that Jesus will judge al nations tell us about His authority?

2. Is it possible for any to reject Jesus and still gain entrance to heaven? Give reasons for your answer.

3. Some say that there are many people who are 'living right' who do not accept Jesus as their Lord but love God. Are such heaven-bound? Please refer to the following texts.

   - John 5:19 – 29
   - Acts 17: 29 – 31
   - I John 2: 23
   - I John 5: 11, 12

Note:

Some, including professing Christians, believe that there are many 'righteous men and women' across the world that do not believe in the Lord Jesus Christ but have 'faith in God'. They subscribe to the erroneous belief that such people are supposedly 'living right' and will therefore gain a place in heaven. Such teaching only helps satan to promote his damnable heresies!

It is important to appraise again the consequence of the Fall. As a result of Adam's fall mankind has been automatically cut off from God the Father. We lost our opportunity in Adam. We lost our inheritance in Adam. We lost our relationship with God in Adam. We lost true fellowship with God in Adam. Yes, we lost our right to heaven in Adam.

However, Jesus Christ, who came in the form of human flesh, lived a sinless life, fulfilled the demands of God and died a sacrificial death as planned by God the Father. As a result, God the Father made Jesus Christ to be the inheritor of all things, including the Kingdom of God.

The only way mankind can ever attain heaven is by accepting Jesus' offer to jointly partake in ***His own inheritance given to Him from the Father*** and this can never be possible if we reject Him. Rejecting Christ, therefore, means to reject the only hope and the only Saviour given to us by God the Father. Through one man, Adam, we are damned and through one man, Jesus Christ, we are saved.

Romans 5: 17 and 19 summarises the above illustration very well: **'For if by one man's (Adam's) offence death reigned by one; much more they which receive abundance of grace and of the gift of righteousness shall reign in life by one, Jesus Christ. For as by one man's disobedience many were made sinners, so by the obedience of one shall many be made righteous.**

4. Read Matthew 25:34. What is the significance of Christ being referred to as 'King'?

5. Please read the following references about Christ's Kingship and discuss:

- Matthew 2:2
- Matthew 21:5
- Matthew 27: 37
- John 1:49
- Revelation 17:14
- Revelation 19: 11 – 16

6. Read Matthew 25: 35, 36, 40. Who were the people Christ was referring to as being hungry, thirsty, strangers, naked, sick and prisoners?

Note:

There is not one account in the Bible where Jesus Christ called the unbelievers or the worldly people His brethren. He used the word 'brethren' to refer to the believers and his own disciples. This is where many wrongly interpret the parable. There are those who take a simplistic reading of this parable and relate it to the needy in the world at large. Nothing could be far from the truth! The fact that a person is poor and is needy does not qualify him or her as a brother or sister of Christ.

As a matter of fact there are many needy people, prisoners, naked and sick people who do not believe in the Lord Jesus Christ and blaspheme His name even in their sordid state. Do their needy conditions make them the brethren of Christ? Absolutely not! Interpreting the parable this way takes out the spiritual import and reduces it to the level of a mere secular injunction.

In addition, there are many philanthropists with very good intentions involved in alleviating the plight of the poor and the needy across the globe. There are also corporations who have very commendable programmes on social responsibility and are reaching out to the disadvantaged within the community.

he question that arises again is, 'Are these good gestures carried out by hilanthropists and corporations sufficient to make them become Jesus' rethren? The answer is 'no!'

uffice to say that there are many philanthropists and corporations who do not ant to hear anything about Jesus Christ. Be very certain that their good estures towards the poor and needy will not take them an inch nearer heaven!

et us always remember to put this parable in perspective. Jesus was speaking bout His Kingdom and of what is expected of the believers in His Kingdom to reach out to the poor and needy believers in His Kingdom. This is why He ses the phrase: 'Inasmuch as you have done it unto one of **the least of these ny brethren (in the Kingdom)**, ye have done it unto me' (Matthew 25:40).

. Read the following references and explain who Christ called brethren on each occasion?

- Mark 3: 31 – 35
- Matthew 23: 8
- Matthew 28: 5 -10
- John 20: 14 – 17

3. Read Matthew 25:37. The word 'righteous' denotes something about the people Christ was referring to. What is it?

9. What is the importance of Matthew 25:40 in relation to Galatians 6:10?

10. Read Matthew 25:41. Hell was not originally prepared for mankind, b
why are many going there?

Note:

This is a very fascinating parable because it once again proves that a casu reading of Scripture will never provide the right interpretation to God's trut no matter how 'simple' the truth might seem. The essence of this parable is t underscore the importance of believers looking out for their fellow brethre (believers) and providing help, support and sustenance at the time of the need.

You will notice that in Matthew 25:44, those referred to as goats, said: 'Lorc when saw we thee an hungered, or athirst, or a stranger, or naked, or sick, c in prison and did not minister to thee?' The fact that they called Jesus 'Lorc shows that these were not ignorant unbelievers but 'church- people' familia with the identity of the Lord Jesus Christ. However, they failed to alleviate th hardship and adversity of brethren even though they had ample opportunity t do so. Simply put they were selfish, uncaring and not Christlike (althoug religious).

It is true that as believers we are expected to help mankind in general wheneve and wherever we can, however, **the primary focus should always be th people of God first** as Galatians 6:10 confirms: ***'As we have therefor opportunity, let us do good unto all men, especially unto them who ar of the household of faith.'*** (Amen)

LESSON 11

THE PROUD SHALL BE BROUGHT LOW
TEXT: Isaiah 14: 12 – 15; Matthew 18: 1 – 4; Micah 6:8

Pride is the oldest sin in the Bible and it is the root from which all other sins sprout. The warning against pride can be found in both the Old and New Testaments. Considering the fact that pride has led to the fall of many (spirit beings and human beings alike), it is imperative that every believer watches very carefully against any sign of pride.

In James 4:6 we are told that God gives grace unto the humble and resists the proud. Pride led to the fall of Lucifer and a third of the heavenly host. Pride led to the sudden death of Herod who was smitten of God. Pride cost Adam and Eve the garden of Eden and the loss of intimate fellowship with the God of heaven. Nebuchadnezzar had a strange experience of being turned into a beast because of pride.

'At the end of twelve months he walked in the palace of the kingdom of Babylon. The king spake, and said, Is not this great Babylon, <u>that I have built for the house of the kingdom by the might of my power, and for the honour of my majesty?</u>

While the word was in the king's mouth, there fell a voice from heaven, saying, O king Nebuchadnezzar, to thee it is spoken; The kingdom is departed from thee. And they shall drive thee from men, and thy dwelling shall be with the beasts of the field: they shall make thee to eat grass as oxen, and seven times shall pass over thee, until thou know that the most High ruleth in the kingdom of men, and giveth it to whomsoever he will.

The same hour was the thing fulfilled upon Nebuchadnezzar: and he was driven from men, and did eat grass as oxen, and his body was wet

with the dew of heaven, till his hairs were grown like eagles' feathers and his nails like birds' claws' (Daniel 4:28–33).

Ahithophel committed suicide because he was too proud to face the fact that his counsel was not accepted by Absalom. In spite of the irrefutable miracles of our Lord Jesus Christ, the Pharisees still rejected Him because they were too proud to submit to His authority and Lordship.

The list of those who have fallen into destruction through pride is endless and sad to say, many are still making the very same mistake of harbouring pride. We must, however, note that pride can be very subtle because in most cases it has to do with the heart's disposition and not just outward actions.

1. Why does God hate pride so much?

2. Read Isaiah 14: 12 – 15 and answer the following questions:

i. From where did pride first arise (i.e. who is the originator of pride)?

ii. Where does pride normally take place in a person?

Note:
It is very important to note that pride usually takes place in the heart! There will be many surprises in eternity! There will be people who did very good deeds of service but with a proud heart neatly tucked away from the eyes of men. You might be surprised to notice that Lucifer's sin was that of the heart. Look again at what the Scripture says:

'For thou hast said <u>in thine heart</u>, I will ascend into heaven…..' (Isaiah 14:13).

Many think that pride can easily be detected by what people do or say. This issue of pride is much deeper than that. It has to do first with the heart! The fact that someone acts righteously, seems to be walking humbly and talking gently does not mean he or she is truly humble. This is why over and over again Scripture says that God ***'tries the heart and the reins'*** (and not mere outward actions).

'But, O LORD of hosts, that judgest righteously, that triest the reins and the heart, (Jeremiah 11:20)

'I the Lord search the heart, I try the reins, even to give every man according his ways, and according to the fruit of his doings (Jeremiah 17:10)

'..I am he which searcheth the reins and hearts: and I will give unto every one of you according to your works (Revelation 2:23).

It is possible for pride to be well hidden away from the eyes of men. However, the searching eyes of God will eventually bring it to light. Then, unfortunately for many, it will be too late to do anything about it. Let us, therefore, ensure that while we have grace, we continually present our hearts before the holy God for purification.

3. According to Scripture, where in particular did sin take place in these references:

   i. Psalm 14:1

   ii. Acts 5:3

   iii. Matthew 15: 18 – 20

4. Compare Genesis 3: 1 – 5 with Luke 4: 5 – 7. Comment on the similarity and on how both temptations point to pride?

5. Please read James 4: 6, 7 and explain the Scripture.

6. What was responsible for the death of Herod in Acts 12: 20 – 23?

7. What warning does Herod's death give us?

8. Read the following references and explain how deadly pride is:

   i. Proverbs 6: 16 – 18

   ii. Proverbs 15:25

   iii. Proverbs 16:5

   iv. Proverbs 11:2

9. Read Proverbs 29:23. Can you give examples of people who were brought low through pride?

10. On the basis of Matthew 18: 1 - 4, what is the pre-requisite for gaining entrance into heaven?

1. How is Micah 6:8 relevant to this lesson on pride?

LESSON 12

SO GREAT A SALVATION: JUSTIFICATION

TEXT: Romans 3: 9 – 31; Romans 5:1, 15 – 21; Galatians 2:16-21

In one of our previous lessons we learnt that our sins have been atoned for b the vicarious death of Jesus Christ's on the Cross. Jesus Christ became ou substitute, He took the penalty for our sins and we are now reconciled wit God. ***'For if, when we were enemies, we were reconciled to God by the death of his Son, much more, being reconciled, we shall be saved by h. life.*** (Romans 5:10).

It is true that we have been reconciled to God through the death of Jesu Christ, but how does God see the believer after reconciliation? What kind c relationship exists between the believer and God after reconciliation? Doe God see us as just forgiven sinners? Does He view us as guilty people merel hanging on to the thread of His divine amnesty? Or does He view us as a acquitted accused?

According to revelation of God's word, the unfathomable riches of God' salvation includes a glorious truth called **'Justification'**. Justification is a divin act of God, whereby He declares the believer to be righteous and just befor Him. The believer's union with Christ is the basis for God's declaration of ou justness and righteousness in His sight. This is so because God now sees th believer through the 'lenses' of Christ's own righteousness.

The most amazing and mind-boggling truth about justification is that God doe not declare the believer to be mere forgiven sinners, rather He looks at us as i we never sinned. Now we may wonder how this is possible. Isn't Goc compromising His holy standard by making this 'bold' declaration that the believer is now just (as if he never sinned)?

To understand justification, we will need to go back once again to wha happened at the cross because this is where the explanation to justification is found. Do you remember when Christ said on the Cross 'My God, my God why hast thou forsaken me?' God the Father forsook His Son because at that moment our sins were 'transferred' to Christ's account and consequently, He had to die. God made Jesus ***to be sin for us, who knew no sin*** (II Corinthians 5:21).

In like manner, the righteousness of Christ has been transferred to the account of everyone that truly believes. What is the value and description of the righteousness transferred into our account? Since it is the righteousness of Christ, it means this righteousness is spotless. This is the righteousness that has never been tainted by sin. This is the righteousness that fulfilled all the demands of the law.

This is the righteousness that God cannot find any fault with and guess what? This righteousness has been transferred to our own account! Praise the Lord! What a glorious salvation indeed! This is why Christ is called **'THE LORD OUR RIGHTEOUSNESS'** (Jeremiah 23:6).

We are not only reconciled to God but also justified in His sight! What grace this is! Hallelujah! May the good Lord give us divine insight and understanding as we study together God's inexplicable declaration of the believer's **'Justification.'**

1. What is the Biblical meaning of Justification?

2. Please read the following scriptures and explain each one in relation to justification.

    - I Corinthians 1: 30

    - Romans 8:30

- Romans 3: 24 – 26
- Galatians 2: 16
- Acts 13: 38, 39

3. One has to possess a certain kind of righteousness that perfectly meets all the standard of God before God can declare such a person to be justified in His sight. What is this righteousness called in Scripture? Please read Romans 3: 21. 22 for your answer.

Note:
It is on the basis of 'The Righteousness of God' that man is declared justified in God's sight. Any other kind of righteousness devised by man will never be able to meet the holy standard of God. It is this 'Righteousness of God' that is transferred to the account of the believer that warrants God to declare him or her as justified in His sight.

But where does this 'Righteousness of God', that is transferred to the believers account, come from? It comes from the life of Jesus Christ's perfect obedience to God while on earth. Scripture tells us that he was ***in all points tempted like as we are yet without sin*** (Hebrews 4:15). In II Corinthians 5:21 we are told that Jesus ***knew no sin***. Apostle Peter confirms that Jesus ***did no sin, neither was guile found in his mouth*** (I Peter 2: 22). In reference to Christ, John the beloved said in his Epistle: ***'And ye know that he was manifested to take away our sins; and in him is no sin'*** (I John 3:5).

Jesus Christ lived in perfect obedience to God without one speckle of sin all through His life. He thereby fulfilled all the righteousness of God to the letter. It is this spotless life of Christ that is called 'The Righteousness of God'. By virtue of this righteousness being transferred to the account of the believer by faith in Jesus Christ, God declares the believer to be justified. This is why Romans 5:19 says that by ***the obedience of one (Jesus) shall many (believers) be made righteous.*** It is this transference of righteousness into our account that is called ***'IMPUTATION'.***

4. The Bible says our sins were imputed to Christ while Christ's righteousness has been imputed to the believer. How does Leviticus 16:20 – 22 help explain the meaning of imputation (the transference of one thing to another person's account)?

Note:

If **'real'** sins where transferred to the account of Jesus Christ which necessitated His **'real'** crucifixion then, in the same vein, **'real'** righteousness has been transferred to the account of the believer, which necessitates our justification before God. Words cannot express the depth, height and breadth of this amazing salvation! ***O the depth of the riches both of the wisdom and knowledge of God! how unsearchable are his judgments, and his ways past finding out!*** (Romans 11:33).

Martin Luther once said: **'For God does not want to save us by our own but by an extraneous righteousness, one that does not originate in ourselves but comes to us from beyond ourselves, which does not arise on earth but comes from heaven.'**

5. Not all kinds of righteousness can justify us before God. Please read the following references and separate the righteousness that justifies from the one that does not.

- Romans 3:21, 22
- Romans 9:31

- Romans 9:30
- Romans 10:3
- Philippians 3:9

6. Read the following references and explain why our own works (our righteousness) cannot justify us before God.

    - Romans 3: 9 - 19
    - Romans 3:23
    - Isaiah 64: 6
    - James 2: 10, 11
    - Isaiah 53: 6

Note:
Man is helpless and destitute of the kind of righteousness demanded by God for our justification. God consequently looks to Himself to produce the kind of righteousness that meets His standard. This is why Isaiah 59:16 says that ***His arm brought salvation unto him*** (through the Lord Jesus Christ). God then transfers this same righteousness to our account for our justification.

Therefore what justifies man in the sight of God is what God Himself has provided, ***that no flesh should glory in His presence*** (I Corinthians 1:29). Jesus Christ ***was delivered for our offences, and was raised again for our justification*** (Romans 4:25).

7. Some find it very difficult to grasp the doctrine of justification by faith, yet this teaching was taught all through the Old Testament. Please read the

following references and explain how 'justification by faith' was taught in the Old Testament.

- Isaiah 53: 11
- Galatians: 3:8
- Galatians 3:21
- Compare Galatians 3: 11 with Habakkuk 2: 4
- Compare Psalm 31: 1,2 with Romans 4: 6 – 8
- Compare Genesis 15: 6 with Romans 4: 1 - 3

Please read Romans 3:20 and explain why God had to devise another means of justifying the believer outside of his own works.

Is justification the same as forgiveness? If not, what is the difference?

0. Please read Romans 5:10. How does this verse capture the doctrine of atonement and justification at the same time?

1. How important is faith in the believer's justification?

Note:
You will notice that the words ***believe, grace, faith, impute and promise*** are used severally in Romans Chapter 4 and they all point to having to trust in

someone apart from ourselves. The repetitive use of these words underscor the fact that, the righteousness God requires of mankind is not the one that w can work out or produce by ourselves. Consequently, mankind, by faith, has look unto someone else to work out this righteousness for him. This Person none other than our Lord and Saviour Jesus Christ.

Faith is the only way of receiving this righteousness and it has become stumbling block to many who want to be the author of their ow righteousness. Instead of submitting to the righteousness of God, they hav gone about to establish their own. This is what happened to Israel as a natio ***But Israel, which followed after the law of righteousness, hath n attained to the law of righteousness. Wherefore? Because they sought not by faith, but as it were by the works of the law. For they stumbled that stumblingstone; As it is written, Behold, I lay in Sion stumblingstone and rock of offence: and whosoever believeth on hi shall not be ashamed.'*** (Romans 9: 31 – 33).

Those who refuse to submit to the righteousness of God by faith manifest th spirit of Cain by carving out a way of righteousness for themselves that i foreign to the righteousness of God. ***For they being ignorant of God righteousness, and going about to establish their own righteousness have not submitted themselves unto the righteousness of God.*** (Roman 10:3).

12. If justification means that Christ's righteousness is transferred to th believer's account, isn't this an encouragement from God to live the way w want? Please read the following references for your answer.

    - Romans 3:28 – 31
    - Romans 6: 1 – 4
    - II Corinthians 5: 14, 15

- I Peter 4: 1, 2

Note:

By virtue of our union with Christ Jesus, we are not only justified but we are regenerated by the Holy Spirit too. This regeneration enables the believer to walk in the newness of life. Consequently, it is not possible for a person to claim justification by faith and live in the old life. Justification is not a path to lawlessness and sinful living. In fact this is quite the opposite. ***Do we then make void the law through faith? God forbid: yea, we establish the law*** (Romans 3:31).

With justification comes regeneration and this is what we will be studying next.

LESSON 13

SO GREAT A SALVATION: REGENERATION

TEXT: John 3: 3 – 8; Ezekiel 36: 25 – 27; II Corinthians 5: 17; Romans 6:4

The wonder of God's saving grace will mean absolutely nothing to the individual, Heaven, the Church and the devil if it is void of that important experience called ***'REGENERATION'***. It is the experience of regeneration that makes the believer stand out as a true witness and a burning light for the Lord Jesus Christ. The only real evidence of having an experiential knowledge of saving grace is regeneration.

Regeneration can be defined as ***'the gracious work of God in the believer's life that quickens him from the deadness of sin and slavery to the old-life, to live a divinely imparted Christ-like life'.*** This definition highlights two important facts;

(1.) Regeneration is divinely imparted.

(2.) The purpose of regeneration is to enable the believer to live righteously in this ungodly world and partake of God's divine nature.

Apostle Peter, in his second epistle (II Peter 1:4) says: **'Whereby are given unto us exceeding great and precious promises: that by these ye might be partakers of the divine nature, having escaped the corruption that is in the world through lust'**

Our profession of faith will remain mere words without regeneration. While atonement and justification are sovereign acts of God done outside of the believer, regeneration is God's work done within the believer. God imparts Christ's life in us that we might walk on earth as Christ walked. Notice what Titus 3: 3 – 5 says:

'For we ourselves also were sometimes foolish, disobedient, deceived, serving divers lusts and pleasures, living in malice and envy, hateful, and hating one another. But after that the kindness and love of God our Saviour toward man appeared, Not by works of righteousness which we have done, but according to his mercy he saved us, by the washing of regeneration, and renewing of the Holy Ghost;'

There are a number of truths reflected in the above reference. Firstly, Titus points out the distinguishing difference between the life before salvation and the one after salvation. This line must never be blurred. The indispensability of an outward difference at the point of salvation is emphasised all through the Bible (to be saved and still walk in the old life is foreign to God and negates Biblical truth).

Secondly, he points out that salvation is the sovereign act of God and has nothing to do with the works of man. This means that regeneration cannot be attained through the works of man. Regeneration is not about striving within ourselves to be better for God through our own powers. No, it is a gift from God. This is how great our salvation is!

The third thing we note is the relationship between salvation and regeneration. This he does to show that regeneration is an integral part of genuine salvation.

1. What is regeneration?

2. What is the difference between God's 'imputation of righteousness' and God's 'impartation of righteousness'?

Note:

'Imputation' is used to describe the transference of Christ's righteousness to the believer's account, while **'Impartation'** is the Christ-like or God-given life imparted to the believer. Imputation is an experience that happens outside the believer, while impartation occurs within the believer. Imputation underscores a change in our standing with God (we now have a right standing with Him). Impartation underscores a change in our lives that results in godly living.

3. How does regeneration differ from atonement and justification?

Apostle James, in some way, refers to the truth about regeneration at salvation in James 2:18, 17 **'Yea, a man may say Thou hast faith, and I have works: shew me thy faith without thy works** ***(a mere confession of Christ or mental assent without the regenerated life)*****, and I will shew thee my faith by my works** ***(the regenerated life that comes from God)'*****.**

The ultimate purpose of the life, death, burial and resurrection of Jesus Christ is that we might henceforth **'walk in the newness of life'** and this can only be experienced at the point of regeneration, which in other words is known as being **'born again'.**

4. Read the following references and explain the terms used to describe regeneration.

    I. John 3: 3, 7 and I Peter 1:23

    II. I John 3:9, 4:7, 5:1, 4, 18

    III. John 3: 6, 8

5. Please read Ezekiel 36: 25 – 27 and explain whether people in the Old Testament experienced regeneration? Give reason for your answers based on this reference.

ote:

n the above reference (Ezekiel 36:25–27) you will notice the phrase ***'a new eart'*** and ***'a new spirit'***. In the Epistles, the word **'new'** is used many times reference to regeneration. II Corinthians 5:17 tells us that the genuine eliever is a ***'new creature'***, we are told to walk in the ***'newness of life'*** in omans 6:4. The believer in Romans 7:6 is admonished to ***'serve in the ewness of spirit'*** and referred to as a ***'new lump'*** in I Corinthians 5:7. phesians 2:15 and Colossians 3:10 calls the believer a ***'new man'***.

Notice what Scripture says in Hebrews 10:19 – 20: **'Having therefore, rethren, boldness to enter into the holiest by the blood of Jesus'. By a ew and living way...'**

his means we cannot enter into the holiest through the **'old way of living'** ut through the 'new way' (the regenerated way). This is the heavenly-way very true child of God receives at salvation.

Regeneration is a change in our moral and spiritual constitution (nature) that ssentially deals with the depravity we inherited from Adam. God does not eave us with this depravity after salvation. At salvation, God takes away this lepravity and, in exchange, gives us the Christ-like nature. This divine operation is what is called **'regeneration'**.

. Is it possible to experience regeneration and still live in the old life? Please refer to the following references for your answer.

- Titus 3: 3 – 8
- Titus 2: 11, 12
- Ephesians 4: 17 – 24

7. What does the Bible say about those who claim to be saved without the evidence of regeneration? Read the references below for your answer.

- I John 2: 6
- Colossians 3: 1 – 6
- Matthew 7: 16 – 20
- Ephesians 2: 1 – 3
- I Corinthians 6: 9 – 11

Note:
The doctrine of 'being saved' without the evidence of regeneration is one c the most damnable heresies satan has successfully injected into the church. Hi strategy seems to be working in many places where people continue to clair salvation without regeneration. Many preach about the greatness of God's lov to forgive while neglecting the greatness of God's power to regenerate our live from a depraved state to that of His divine nature.

In fact, when Apostle Peter talks about the greatness of salvation, he does s in relation to the divine nature God gives to all who are truly converted an not just in relation to God's forgiveness.

'According as his divine power hath given unto us all things that pertai unto life and godliness, through the knowledge of him that hath calle us to glory and virtue: Whereby are given unto us exceeding great an precious promises: that by these ye might be partakers of the divin nature, having escaped the corruption that is in the world through lust.
– II Peter 1:3, 4

From the above Scripture, we discover the following;

- There is a link between God's divine power and the receiving of God's divine nature. Those who receive the divine nature do so as a result of

- God's intervening power. Where there is intervening power from above (grace), there will be the God-given life on earth (regeneration).

- There is an inseparable link between salvation and godliness (regeneration).

- The experience of regeneration comes through proper knowledge (teaching) of our Lord and Saviour Jesus Christ. This means if we truly know Him we will experience regeneration irrespective of what others teach or believe.

- God's promises in relation to the divine nature (regeneration) are considered great and exceeding in His sight. This is why our salvation is called **'so great a salvation'**.

- The end-result of being recipients of the divine nature (regeneration) is that we will no longer remain in bondage to the corruption of this present evil world.

What great a salvation the Lord has wrought for us! What terrible loss not to experience the fullness of so great a salvation! The Lord's desire is that we are filled with the fullness of God! (Ephesians 3:19). Unfortunately, many in the church are listening to satan's teaching and to doctrine of devils. Consequently, they pitch their tents far away from the glorious experience of regeneration. Many simply prefer to cling to a 'gospel of forgiveness' without regeneration.

That kind of gospel is taught nowhere in Scripture and does not lead to eternal life.

8. What are the dangers of believing a 'gospel of forgiveness' without regeneration?

9. In spite of God's 'great and exceeding' promise called regeneration, many in the church do not experience it. Why is this so?

10. Please read II Corinthians 5:17 and Galatians 5:24 and explain how regeneration is both an integral part and proof of genuine salvation.

11. What is the end result of regeneration according to Ezekiel 36: 27?

Note:
The radical change that occurs in the believer at 'regeneration' is so amazing and irrefutable that the believer's transformed life becomes a testimony in itself. This is what Paul the Apostle underscored when referring to the brethren at Thessalonica (I Thessalonians 1:5–9). Jesus Christ said: **'Let your light so shine before men, that they may see your good works, and glorify your Father which is in heaven'.** This can only happen through the power of God at regeneration. Regeneration empowers us to walk in the ***'newness of life'*** and is a gift received at salvation through faith.

The end-result of having a **'new heart'** and **'a new spirit'** (regeneration), is the grace to walk in God's statutes. Regeneration causes the believer **'to walk in (His) statutes, and keep my (His) judgements, and do them' – Ezekiel 36: 26, 27.**

12. Read Ephesians 2: 1 – 10 and point out how the doctrine of regeneration is contained therein.

Why not start a home group and be an instrument of revival in your locality? You have the material right in your hands. Furthermore, if you will like to be part of the International Home Bible Fellowship, streamed live to believers across the world weekly, you can go to our YouTube Channel called **'The National Home Bible Fellowship'.** For more information email info@samsonjebutu.com or call our 24hour line: +44 (0)2087 980 961

Printed in Great Britain
by Amazon

27466237R00051